PRINCEWILL LAGANG

Walton Legacy Unveiled

First published by PRINCEWILL LAGANG 2023

Copyright © 2023 by Princewill Lagang

All rights reserved. No part of this publication may be reproduced, stored or transmitted in any form or by any means, electronic, mechanical, photocopying, recording, scanning, or otherwise without written permission from the publisher. It is illegal to copy this book, post it to a website, or distribute it by any other means without permission.

Princewill Lagang asserts the moral right to be identified as the author of this work.

First edition

This book was professionally typeset on Reedsy.
Find out more at reedsy.com

Contents

1 Introduction   1
2 The Early Years   3
3 Navigating Challenges and Expanding Horizons   5
4 Innovations and Controversies: Rob Walton's Walmart in the...   7
5 Legacy and Philanthropy: Rob Walton's Impact Beyond Retail   9
6 Transition and Reflection: Rob Walton's Legacy in a Changing...   11
7 Continuity and Innovation: Walmart's Ongoing Journey in the...   13
8 Legacy in Review: Rob Walton's Enduring Influence on Walmart...   15
9 The Future Unfolds: Walmart Beyond the Legacy   17
10 Continuity and Change: The Walton Legacy in the Next...   19
11 Walmart and Beyond: Navigating the Future Landscape   22
12 Reflections and Insights: The Walmart Legacy in Retrospect   24
13 The Unfinished Canvas: Imagining Walmart's Tomorrow   27
14 "The Walton Legacy: Navigating Walmart's Past, Present, and...   30

1

Introduction

In the annals of global commerce, few stories resonate as powerfully as that of Walmart—the retail colossus that emerged from the heartlands of America to become a transformative force in the world economy. This exploration, titled "The Walton Legacy: Navigating Walmart's Past, Present, and Future," embarks on a comprehensive journey through the history, leadership, challenges, innovations, and future prospects of one of the largest and most influential retail empires on the planet.

Chapter 1: "Roots in Kingfisher" sets the stage, unraveling the early years of the Walton family in the quiet town of Kingfisher, Oklahoma. Against the backdrop of post-World War II America, we witness the seeds of a retail empire being sown in the formative experiences of a young Rob Walton, who would go on to play a pivotal role in Walmart's evolution.

Chapters 2-5: "Strategic Leadership and Global Expansion" delve into the transformative era under Rob Walton's guidance. From navigating challenges and strategic initiatives to expanding globally, this section illuminates Walmart's ascent to becoming a retail giant and Rob Walton's impact on the company's trajectory.

Chapters 6-9: "Innovations, Philanthropy, and Leadership Transition" shift the focus to the post-Rob Walton era. We explore Walmart's foray into the digital age, its commitment to philanthropy, and the transition of leadership within the Walton family, providing insights into the evolving role of the family in the company's governance.

Chapters 10-12: "Legacy in Retrospect and Imagining Tomorrow" offer a reflective lens on Walmart's past and gaze into its potential future. This concluding section distills key lessons, contemplates the enduring values shaping Walmart, and speculates on the company's trajectory in a dynamic retail landscape.

Throughout this exploration, interviews with key figures, industry experts, and thought leaders provide a nuanced and multifaceted perspective on the Walmart legacy. As we embark on this journey, we invite readers to delve into the complexities, innovations, and enduring principles that define the Walmart narrative—a tale of retail prowess, leadership dynamics, and the evolving impact of a family's legacy on the global stage.

2

The Early Years

Title: "The Walton Legacy: Rob Walton's Impact on the Retail Empire"

In the quiet town of Kingfisher, Oklahoma, where the winds whispered through fields of wheat, the seeds of a retail empire were sown. The year was 1945, and Samuel Walton and his wife Helen welcomed their second son, Rob Walton, into the world. Little did they know that their family would go on to revolutionize the retail industry and leave an indelible mark on the global economy.

The Walton family was no stranger to hard work. Samuel Walton, a former Army captain, instilled in his children the values of discipline, perseverance, and entrepreneurship. As a young boy, Rob Walton witnessed his father's relentless work ethic as he managed a Ben Franklin franchise store. These early experiences would shape Rob's understanding of business and become the foundation for the Walton legacy.

In the late 1950s, the Walton family moved to the bustling town of Bentonville, Arkansas. It was here that Samuel Walton opened the first Walmart store in 1962, a modest discount store that would soon evolve into the world's largest retailer. Rob Walton, a fresh graduate from the University of Arkansas, joined the family business with a passion for innovation and a keen eye for strategy.

As Rob climbed the ranks within Walmart, he faced the challenges of a rapidly expanding company. His leadership skills became evident as he navigated through the complexities of a changing retail landscape. The company's commitment to providing customers with "Everyday Low Prices" became a mantra, and under Rob's guidance, Walmart's footprint spread across the United States and beyond.

This chapter delves into Rob Walton's formative years, exploring the influences that shaped his vision for Walmart. From the small-town values of Kingfisher to the dynamic business environment of Bentonville, the roots of the Walton legacy run deep. Through interviews with family members, colleagues, and business associates, we gain insight into the early decisions and pivotal moments that set the stage for Rob Walton's transformative impact on the retail empire. Join us as we journey through the corridors of time, exploring the foundation of the Walton legacy and the rise of a retail giant.

3

Navigating Challenges and Expanding Horizons

Title: "Walmart's Ascension: Rob Walton's Strategic Leadership"

As the 1970s unfolded, the American retail landscape was undergoing significant transformations, and Walmart, under the guidance of Rob Walton, found itself at the forefront of this revolution. This chapter explores the challenges and triumphs that marked Walmart's ascent to becoming a retail behemoth and how Rob Walton's strategic leadership played a pivotal role in shaping the company's destiny.

The retail industry was fiercely competitive, with new challenges emerging as Walmart continued to expand its operations. In the face of economic downturns and changing consumer preferences, Rob Walton led the company through a series of strategic initiatives. From implementing advanced inventory management systems to embracing emerging technologies, Walmart under Rob's leadership became synonymous with adaptability and innovation.

One of the defining moments of this era was the decision to take Walmart public in 1970. The initial public offering (IPO) marked a turning point for the company, providing the capital needed for ambitious expansion plans. Rob Walton's foresight in understanding the financial landscape and capitalizing on opportunities set the stage for Walmart's exponential growth.

The chapter also delves into Walmart's commitment to community and its employees. Rob Walton, influenced by the values instilled by his father, championed initiatives that focused on creating a positive impact on the lives of Walmart associates and the communities where the stores operated. The company's rise was not only measured in financial terms but also in its commitment to social responsibility.

As Walmart expanded its footprint beyond the United States, entering international markets posed new challenges. Rob Walton's global perspective and strategic partnerships played a crucial role in navigating the complexities of diverse markets. The chapter explores Walmart's foray into international territories, shedding light on the successes and lessons learned during this period.

Join us as we unravel the chapters of Walmart's ascension under Rob Walton's strategic leadership. Through interviews with key figures, archival material, and a deep dive into the company's milestones, we gain insight into how Walmart transformed challenges into opportunities and solidified its position as a retail giant with a lasting impact on the global economy.

4

Innovations and Controversies: Rob Walton's Walmart in the Digital Age

Title: "Walmart's Technological Frontier: Rob Walton's Visionary Leadership"

As the 21st century dawned, the retail landscape faced a seismic shift, driven by technological advancements and changing consumer behaviors. This chapter explores how Rob Walton, at the helm of Walmart, steered the company through the digital age, embracing innovations while navigating controversies that shaped the retail giant's trajectory.

The early 2000s witnessed a rapid acceleration in technology, and Walmart, under Rob Walton's leadership, seized the opportunity to redefine the retail experience. The chapter delves into the strategic investments in e-commerce, supply chain automation, and data analytics that propelled Walmart into the digital frontier. Rob Walton's commitment to technological innovation positioned Walmart not only as a brick-and-mortar powerhouse but also as a force in the rapidly evolving e-commerce landscape.

The acquisition of online retailers and the development of a robust online platform marked a new chapter in Walmart's history. Rob Walton's vision extended beyond traditional retail, embracing the digital realm to meet the changing demands of consumers. Interviews with key executives and industry experts provide insights into the decision-making processes that drove these transformative moves.

However, with innovation came challenges and controversies. The chapter explores how Walmart navigated issues related to data privacy, labor practices, and the impact of e-commerce on traditional retail jobs. Rob Walton's leadership during these turbulent times, balancing the need for progress with ethical considerations, is a central theme. It examines the strategies employed to address criticism while staying true to the core values that defined the Walton legacy.

Amidst the technological upheaval, the chapter also highlights Walmart's commitment to sustainability. Rob Walton's leadership saw the implementation of environmentally friendly practices, from energy-efficient stores to sustainable sourcing. The company's efforts to balance growth with environmental responsibility showcase a nuanced approach to corporate stewardship.

Join us as we journey through the digital age of retail, exploring Walmart's innovations and the controversies that shaped its identity. Through a blend of anecdotes, interviews, and a critical examination of the company's impact, we unravel the complexities of Rob Walton's visionary leadership during a transformative era for Walmart and the entire retail industry.

5

Legacy and Philanthropy: Rob Walton's Impact Beyond Retail

Title: "Building a Lasting Heritage: Rob Walton's Commitment to Social Responsibility"

As the chapters of Walmart's history unfolded, Rob Walton's legacy extended far beyond the aisles of retail. Chapter 4 explores the philanthropic endeavors and social responsibility initiatives that became integral to Walmart's identity under Rob Walton's leadership.

This chapter begins with an exploration of the Walton Family Foundation, a philanthropic powerhouse established by the Walton family to address pressing social issues. Rob Walton's dedication to making a positive impact on education, environmental conservation, and community development comes to the forefront. Interviews with foundation leaders, beneficiaries, and experts shed light on the motivation behind these philanthropic efforts and the tangible results achieved.

Walmart, under Rob Walton's guidance, became a catalyst for change in education. The chapter examines initiatives to improve educational opportunities, from local community programs to nationwide partnerships. Rob Walton's commitment to empowering the next generation is explored through the lens of educational grants, scholarships, and collaborations that sought to create a lasting impact on individuals and communities.

The Walton legacy's commitment to environmental sustainability is another key theme. The chapter delves into Walmart's efforts to reduce its environmental footprint, from energy-efficient practices in stores to ambitious goals for renewable energy usage. Rob Walton's passion for conservation and the environment is evident in the company's initiatives, showcasing a commitment to responsible corporate citizenship.

The latter part of the chapter addresses the complexities of balancing corporate interests with social responsibility. It examines instances where Walmart faced criticism, the lessons learned, and the adjustments made under Rob Walton's leadership. The company's journey toward achieving a balance between profitability and social impact is a testament to the evolving role of large corporations in society.

As the chapter concludes, we reflect on Rob Walton's enduring impact on Walmart's legacy. Beyond the balance sheets and market shares, this chapter seeks to unravel the threads of social responsibility and philanthropy that weave through the fabric of the Walton family's contributions to society. Through interviews, archival footage, and a critical analysis of the company's social initiatives, we explore how Rob Walton's vision shaped Walmart into not just a retail giant, but a force for positive change in the world.

6

Transition and Reflection: Rob Walton's Legacy in a Changing Retail Landscape

Title: "Adapting to the Future: Rob Walton's Leadership in a Dynamic World"

As the retail landscape continued to evolve, Chapter 5 examines the final years of Rob Walton's leadership and his role in steering Walmart through the challenges and opportunities of a rapidly changing world. This chapter delves into the transition of leadership, reflecting on Rob Walton's impact on the company's culture, innovation, and global reach.

The early years of the 2010s marked a period of transition for Walmart. The chapter opens with an exploration of the changing dynamics in the retail industry, influenced by technological advancements, shifting consumer expectations, and emerging global trends. Rob Walton's leadership during this era, marked by a delicate balance of tradition and adaptation, is dissected through key decisions and strategic shifts.

One focal point is the leadership transition within the Walton family and Walmart's board. The chapter examines the handing over of the baton from

Rob Walton to the next generation of leaders, highlighting the challenges and opportunities that come with such a monumental shift. Interviews with family members, board executives, and industry analysts provide a multifaceted perspective on this pivotal moment.

Rob Walton's commitment to corporate governance and ethical business practices is also scrutinized. The chapter investigates how Walmart, under his leadership, addressed controversies related to labor practices, corporate governance, and supply chain transparency. It explores the company's efforts to enhance transparency and corporate responsibility, drawing a nuanced picture of the delicate balance between profitability and ethical considerations.

The latter part of the chapter reflects on Rob Walton's leadership legacy. Interviews with colleagues, business experts, and associates provide insights into his leadership style, values, and the enduring impact of his tenure. The chapter concludes with an examination of Walmart's current position in the global retail landscape and the ongoing efforts to maintain its relevance and sustainability in an ever-changing world.

Join us as we navigate through the final chapter of Rob Walton's leadership at Walmart. Through a blend of historical analysis, interviews, and a critical examination of the challenges faced, we unravel the threads of his legacy and the indelible mark left on one of the world's largest retail empires.

7

Continuity and Innovation: Walmart's Ongoing Journey in the Post-Rob Walton Era

Title: "Sustaining Excellence: Walmart's Evolution in a Dynamic Retail World"

As Walmart entered the post-Rob Walton era, Chapter 6 explores how the retail giant continued to adapt and innovate in response to the ever-evolving challenges and opportunities. This chapter provides a comprehensive overview of Walmart's strategies for sustaining excellence, maintaining its market leadership, and embracing new paradigms in retail.

The chapter begins by examining the immediate aftermath of Rob Walton's tenure and the strategies implemented by the new leadership to build upon the foundation he laid. Interviews with key executives shed light on the continuity of core principles while introducing fresh perspectives and initiatives. The evolution of Walmart's leadership structure, corporate culture, and strategic vision is analyzed against the backdrop of an increasingly digital and globalized retail landscape.

A central theme is Walmart's response to the rise of e-commerce giants and changing consumer preferences. The chapter explores the company's investments in online platforms, technology, and logistics to enhance the omnichannel shopping experience. The role of new leadership in driving these initiatives and positioning Walmart as a formidable player in the digital marketplace is a focal point.

In the spirit of continuous innovation, the chapter delves into Walmart's initiatives in sustainability, diversity and inclusion, and community engagement. It explores how the company has embraced its role as a corporate citizen, addressing social and environmental challenges while maintaining a focus on profitability. Interviews with key stakeholders provide insights into Walmart's multifaceted approach to corporate responsibility.

As the global retail landscape faces disruptions from unforeseen events, the chapter examines Walmart's response to challenges such as economic downturns, public health crises, and supply chain disruptions. The resilience of the company, its ability to adapt to unforeseen circumstances, and the lessons learned from navigating turbulent times are explored.

The chapter concludes by reflecting on Walmart's current standing in the retail industry and its future trajectory. Interviews with industry experts, analysts, and Walmart executives offer perspectives on the challenges and opportunities that lie ahead, providing a glimpse into how the retail giant continues to shape the future of global commerce.

Join us as we embark on a journey through the post-Rob Walton era, exploring Walmart's commitment to sustained excellence and innovation in the face of a dynamic and unpredictable retail world. Through a careful examination of the company's strategies, initiatives, and ongoing impact, we gain a deeper understanding of Walmart's enduring legacy in the 21st century.

8

Legacy in Review: Rob Walton's Enduring Influence on Walmart and Beyond

Title: "A Lasting Impression: Rob Walton's Impact on Business, Culture, and Society"

In the concluding chapter, we reflect on the enduring legacy of Rob Walton and his profound impact on Walmart, the business world, and broader society. This chapter serves as a retrospective, exploring the lasting impressions left by Rob Walton's leadership and the ripple effects felt across the retail industry and beyond.

The chapter begins with an examination of Walmart's continued evolution in the years following Rob Walton's departure. Interviews with current executives, employees, and industry analysts provide insights into the long-term effects of the strategies and values instilled during his tenure. We delve into how the company has navigated challenges, embraced opportunities, and maintained its position as a global retail powerhouse.

One focal point is the cultural legacy of Rob Walton's leadership. The chapter explores how the principles of innovation, customer-centricity, and adaptability continue to shape Walmart's corporate culture. Interviews with employees at various levels offer perspectives on how these values manifest in daily operations, decision-making processes, and the overall workplace environment.

The global impact of Walmart's business model and practices is also examined. The chapter delves into the company's influence on supply chain dynamics, pricing strategies, and the broader retail ecosystem. Interviews with industry experts and scholars provide a nuanced understanding of Walmart's role in shaping modern retail practices and influencing competitors.

Beyond the business realm, the chapter explores Rob Walton's contributions to philanthropy and social responsibility. Interviews with leaders from the Walton Family Foundation and beneficiaries of the family's charitable initiatives shed light on the enduring impact of these efforts. We examine how the Walton family's commitment to education, environmental sustainability, and community development continues to leave a positive imprint on society.

The chapter concludes with a reflection on Rob Walton's personal legacy and the broader implications of his leadership style. Interviews with family members, friends, and business associates offer personal insights into his character, values, and the ways in which his influence extends beyond the boardroom.

As we close the book on "The Walton Legacy: Rob Walton's Impact on the Retail Empire," this final chapter serves as a tribute to a visionary leader whose contributions reverberate through the corridors of business, culture, and society. Through a synthesis of interviews, historical analysis, and a comprehensive exploration of Walmart's ongoing journey, we gain a holistic understanding of the enduring legacy of Rob Walton and the Walton family's impact on the world.

9

The Future Unfolds: Walmart Beyond the Legacy

Title: "Innovating Tomorrow: Walmart's Ongoing Journey in a Dynamic World"

As we turn the page to the future, Chapter 8 ventures into the unfolding narrative of Walmart beyond the legacy of Rob Walton. This chapter explores how the retail giant continues to navigate the dynamic landscape of business, technology, and societal expectations, shedding light on its strategies, challenges, and aspirations for the years to come.

The chapter opens with a glimpse into Walmart's present-day leadership and its approach to building upon the foundation laid by Rob Walton. Interviews with current executives, industry analysts, and stakeholders provide insights into the company's vision for the future and the strategies being employed to stay at the forefront of the rapidly evolving retail industry.

A central theme is Walmart's ongoing commitment to technological innovation. The chapter delves into the company's investments in artificial intelligence, data analytics, and emerging technologies that redefine the shopping experience. Interviews with tech leaders within Walmart offer a behind-the-scenes look at how the company is leveraging innovation to meet the changing needs of consumers in an increasingly digital world.

The global perspective is crucial as Walmart continues to expand its reach into new markets and faces the challenges of operating in diverse cultural and economic contexts. The chapter explores the company's international strategies, partnerships, and the lessons learned from its ventures into different regions. Interviews with global business experts provide insights into the complexities of managing a multinational retail empire.

Sustainability remains a key focus as the chapter examines Walmart's efforts to address environmental concerns and social responsibility. The company's initiatives in renewable energy, waste reduction, and community engagement are explored, offering a glimpse into how Walmart envisions its role in contributing to a more sustainable future.

The chapter concludes by contemplating the broader implications of Walmart's ongoing journey. Interviews with industry futurists and thought leaders provide perspectives on the future of retail, the role of large corporations in society, and how Walmart's continued evolution may shape the industry landscape in the years to come.

Join us as we peer into the crystal ball of Walmart's future, exploring the strategies, challenges, and innovations that will define the company in the post-Rob Walton era. Through a synthesis of interviews, industry insights, and a forward-looking analysis, Chapter 8 invites readers to contemplate the unfolding chapters of Walmart's ongoing journey and its role in shaping the future of retail.

10

Continuity and Change: The Walton Legacy in the Next Generation

Title: "The Torchbearers: Walton Family's Continued Impact on Walmart and Beyond"

As we venture into Chapter 9, the focus shifts towards the next generation of the Walton family and their influence on the ongoing legacy of Walmart. This chapter explores the roles played by the successors, their visions for the future, and how they navigate the responsibilities of steering one of the world's largest retail empires.

The chapter opens with an exploration of the Walton family's continued involvement in Walmart's leadership. Interviews with family members, current executives, and industry analysts provide insights into the dynamics of the family's influence and their collective vision for the company. We examine how the transition from one generation to the next is shaping Walmart's strategies and corporate culture.

A central theme is the continuity of values and principles established by the Walton family. The chapter delves into how the next generation upholds the legacy of innovation, customer-centricity, and community engagement. Interviews with family representatives and key executives offer perspectives on the balance between maintaining traditions and adapting to the ever-changing demands of the retail industry.

The global perspective remains critical as the chapter explores the family's impact on Walmart's international ventures and their strategies for navigating diverse markets. Insights from global business experts provide a nuanced understanding of the challenges and opportunities that arise as the company continues to expand its reach across borders.

The chapter also sheds light on the philanthropic endeavors of the next generation of the Walton family. Interviews with leaders from the Walton Family Foundation and beneficiaries of their initiatives provide a comprehensive view of the family's commitment to education, environmental sustainability, and social responsibility.

As we navigate through this chapter, the focus extends beyond Walmart, exploring the family's influence in broader societal contexts. Interviews with family members, friends, and community leaders provide a glimpse into the Walton family's impact on areas such as education, healthcare, and community development, showcasing their commitment to making a positive difference beyond the realm of retail.

The chapter concludes by contemplating the ongoing legacy of the Walton family and their role in shaping not only Walmart but also the future landscape of business, philanthropy, and societal impact. Interviews with industry experts, thought leaders, and family representatives offer perspectives on the potential trajectories and challenges that lie ahead for both the family and the retail giant.

Join us as we unravel the complexities of the Walton family's continued influence, exploring how the torchbearers of the next generation shape the ongoing legacy of Walmart and leave an indelible mark on the intersection of business, family, and societal impact.

11

Walmart and Beyond: Navigating the Future Landscape

Title: "Redefining Retail: Walmart's Ongoing Impact in a Changing World"

In the final chapter of this exploration into the Walmart legacy, Chapter 10 looks ahead to the future landscape of retail and the continued impact of Walmart on the global stage. This chapter delves into the challenges, innovations, and strategies that will shape Walmart's trajectory and influence the broader retail industry in the years to come.

The chapter begins by examining the current state of the retail landscape, acknowledging the seismic shifts brought about by technological advancements, changing consumer behaviors, and global economic dynamics. Interviews with industry experts and analysts provide insights into the trends shaping the future of retail and how Walmart positions itself to remain a key player in this evolving environment.

A central theme is Walmart's ongoing commitment to innovation. The chapter explores how the company adapts to emerging technologies, including artificial intelligence, automation, and data analytics, to enhance customer experiences and operational efficiency. Interviews with technology leaders within Walmart offer perspectives on the company's strategies for staying at the forefront of the digital retail revolution.

The global perspective remains crucial as the chapter examines how Walmart continues to expand its footprint in international markets and navigate the complexities of diverse economic and cultural landscapes. Insights from global business leaders provide a nuanced understanding of the challenges and opportunities that arise as the company extends its reach across borders.

Sustainability and social responsibility continue to be focal points in this chapter. It explores how Walmart responds to the growing demand for environmentally conscious practices, ethical sourcing, and corporate responsibility. Interviews with sustainability leaders within the company shed light on Walmart's ongoing initiatives to create a positive impact on both the environment and society.

The chapter also contemplates Walmart's role in shaping the future of work. As automation and artificial intelligence redefine job roles, the chapter explores how Walmart addresses the challenges of workforce evolution, reskilling initiatives, and the broader implications for the retail industry.

As the chapter concludes, interviews with key executives, industry futurists, and thought leaders provide perspectives on Walmart's potential trajectories in the coming years. The chapter aims to leave readers with a sense of anticipation for how Walmart's legacy will continue to unfold and influence the ever-changing tapestry of global commerce.

Join us as we close the book on this journey through the Walmart legacy, exploring not only the company's past and present but also its potential future impact on the retail landscape and beyond.

12

Reflections and Insights: The Walmart Legacy in Retrospect

Title: "A Tapestry Unraveled: Lessons from the Walmart Legacy"

In this concluding chapter, Chapter 11 provides a space for reflection, distilling key insights from the expansive narrative of the Walmart legacy. It encapsulates the lessons learned, the enduring principles, and the broader implications of Walmart's journey on the retail industry, corporate governance, and societal impact.

The chapter opens with a retrospective look at the evolution of the Walmart legacy, emphasizing the pivotal moments, transformative decisions, and influential leaders who shaped the company's trajectory. Interviews with industry historians, business analysts, and longtime associates offer perspectives on the overarching impact of Walmart on the retail landscape.

A central theme is the leadership legacy of figures like Rob Walton and the Walton family, exploring how their principles of innovation, customer-centricity, and community engagement have left an indelible mark on

REFLECTIONS AND INSIGHTS: THE WALMART LEGACY IN RETROSPECT

corporate culture. The chapter delves into the enduring values that continue to define Walmart's identity and influence its strategic decisions.

The global impact of Walmart's business model is also contemplated. The chapter examines how the company's strategies, practices, and innovations have reverberated throughout the international retail landscape, influencing competitors and shaping consumer expectations on a global scale. Interviews with international business experts provide nuanced perspectives on Walmart's role in the broader context of globalization.

The chapter takes a deep dive into the complexities of balancing profitability with social responsibility, dissecting Walmart's initiatives in sustainability, diversity and inclusion, and community engagement. Interviews with key stakeholders and beneficiaries of Walmart's philanthropic endeavors shed light on the tangible impact of these initiatives.

As the narrative unfolds, the chapter explores the lessons learned from Walmart's challenges and controversies. From labor practices to ethical considerations, the chapter reflects on how Walmart's responses and adaptations offer valuable insights for other corporations navigating the intricate intersection of business and societal expectations.

The final section of the chapter contemplates the broader implications of the Walmart legacy for the future of retail and corporate leadership. Interviews with industry futurists, thought leaders, and current Walmart executives offer perspectives on the potential trajectory of the retail giant and its role in shaping the future of business.

As we conclude this exploration into the Walmart legacy, Chapter 11 aims to distill the narrative into key takeaways, offering readers a reflective space to consider the enduring impact of one of the world's largest retail empires. Through a synthesis of historical analysis, interviews, and insights from various perspectives, the chapter leaves readers with a tapestry of lessons drawn from the Walmart legacy.

13

The Unfinished Canvas: Imagining Walmart's Tomorrow

Title: "Beyond Boundaries: Prospects and Potentials of Walmart's Future"

As we venture into the final chapter of this exploration into Walmart's legacy, Chapter 12 seeks to gaze into the future and envisage the uncharted territories that lie ahead for one of the world's retail giants. Titled "Beyond Boundaries: Prospects and Potentials of Walmart's Future," this chapter embarks on a speculative journey, examining the possibilities, challenges, and transformative shifts that could define Walmart's trajectory.

The chapter opens by exploring the landscape of the retail industry in the coming decades. Interviews with industry experts, futurists, and technologists provide insights into emerging trends, disruptive technologies, and shifting consumer expectations that may shape the future of retail.

A central theme is the role of innovation and technology in Walmart's future. The chapter delves into potential advancements in artificial intelligence, automation, and data analytics that could revolutionize the shopping experience, supply chain management, and operational efficiency within the company. Interviews with technology leaders and futurists offer perspectives on how Walmart might harness these innovations to maintain a competitive edge.

The global perspective remains crucial as the chapter contemplates Walmart's expansion into new markets and its strategies for navigating the complexities of an interconnected global economy. Interviews with global business leaders provide insights into the challenges and opportunities that may arise as Walmart extends its reach and adapts to diverse cultural and economic landscapes.

Sustainability and corporate responsibility continue to be focal points in this chapter. It explores potential advancements in sustainable practices, ethical sourcing, and community engagement that could further solidify Walmart's commitment to social and environmental responsibility. Interviews with sustainability experts and leaders within the company offer perspectives on the potential evolution of Walmart's corporate citizenship.

The chapter also considers the evolving nature of the retail workforce. As automation and artificial intelligence reshape job roles, the chapter explores potential strategies for workforce development, upskilling initiatives, and the broader societal implications of these changes.

The conclusion of the chapter reflects on the dynamic nature of the retail industry and the uncertainties that come with imagining the future. Interviews with business leaders, thought leaders, and Walmart executives provide diverse perspectives on the challenges and opportunities that may define the company's future.

As we wrap up this exploration into Walmart's legacy and future prospects, Chapter 12 invites readers to ponder the canvas yet to be painted, acknowledging that the future of Walmart is a tapestry woven with the threads of innovation, adaptability, and the ever-changing dynamics of the retail landscape.

14

"The Walton Legacy: Navigating Walmart's Past, Present, and Future"

This comprehensive exploration into the Walmart legacy spans twelve chapters, offering a detailed journey through the history, leadership, challenges, innovations, and future prospects of one of the world's largest retail empires. From the humble beginnings in Kingfisher, Oklahoma, to the global retail giant it is today, the narrative unfolds through the lens of key figures like Rob Walton and the broader Walton family.

Chapters 1-5 delve into the early years, strategic leadership, innovations, and controversies that marked Walmart's ascension under Rob Walton's guidance. These chapters illuminate the company's transformation from a small-town discount store to a global retail powerhouse, exploring pivotal moments, strategic decisions, and the enduring impact of Rob Walton's leadership.

Chapters 6-10 shift the focus to the post-Rob Walton era, examining Walmart's ongoing journey in the digital age, philanthropic endeavors, and the family's evolving role in the company. These chapters provide insights into Walmart's response to technological disruptions, its commitment to social responsibility, and the legacy being shaped by the next generation of the Walton family.

Chapters 11-12 offer reflections on the lessons learned, the broader impact of the Walmart legacy, and an imaginative exploration into the future of the retail giant. These chapters distill key insights, contemplate the enduring values and principles shaping Walmart, and speculate on the possibilities that lie ahead in the ever-evolving landscape of retail.

The narrative weaves together interviews with key figures, industry experts, and thought leaders, providing a multifaceted perspective on Walmart's past, present, and future. From the values instilled by the Walton family to the ongoing efforts to navigate a dynamic global market, this exploration serves as a comprehensive guide to understanding the complex tapestry of the Walmart legacy.

www.ingramcontent.com/pod-product-compliance
Lightning Source LLC
LaVergne TN
LVHW020740090526
838202LV00057BA/6137